DATE			
JUL 14 2008			

The Human Body

The Respiratory System

CHECKERBOARD SCIENCE LIBRARY

THE HUMAN BODY

Kristin Petrie MS, RD • ABDO Publishing Company

visit us at
www.abdopublishing.com

Published by ABDO Publishing Company, 4940 Viking Drive, Edina, Minnesota 55435.
Copyright © 2007 by Abdo Consulting Group, Inc. International copyrights reserved in all
countries. No part of this book may be reproduced in any form without written permission from
the publisher. The Checkerboard Library™ is a trademark and logo of ABDO Publishing Company.

Printed in the United States.

Cover Photo: Corbis
Interior Photos: © Articulate Graphics/Custom Medical Stock Photo pp. 5, 21;
     © Birmingham/Custom Medical Stock Photo p. 6; © Carson/Custom Medical Stock Photo p. 9;
     © Cavallini/Custom Medical Stock Photo p. 27; Corbis pp. 1, 4, 8, 16, 29; Getty Images pp. 7,
     10, 11, 18-19, 22, 23, 25; Index Stock p. 13; © Litwak/Custom Medical Stock Photo p. 19;
     © R.Lazarus/Custom Medical Stock Photo pp. 17, 26-27; Visuals Unlimited pp. 12, 14, 15

Series Coordinator: Heidi M. Dahmes
Editors: Heidi M. Dahmes, Megan Murphy
Art Direction: Neil Klinepier

Library of Congress Cataloging-in-Publication Data

Petrie, Kristin, 1970-
    The respiratory system / Kristin Petrie.
        p. cm. -- (The human body)
    Includes index.
    ISBN-10 1-59679-713-4
    ISBN-13 978-1-59679-713-0
    1. Respiratory organs--Juvenile literature. 2. Respiration--Juvenile literature. I. Title.

QP121.P45 2006
612.2--dc22
                                                                    2005048320

CONTENTS

WHY BREATHE?

Can you name one thing that everyone you know is doing right now? Breathing! Well, maybe some people are holding their breath. But not for long. Everyone needs to inhale and exhale all day and all night.

Why do we need to breathe? Breathing brings oxygen inside our bodies. It also gets rid of carbon dioxide. This exchange of gases keeps us alive.

Respiration describes two processes of your respiratory system. One is the movements your body

You can't hold your breath underwater forever! Your body needs oxygen to keep you swimming.

makes that result in breathing. The other is what your body does with oxygen that it takes in.

Respiration includes getting oxygen into your cells. It is also how your cells use oxygen for fuel. Lastly, respiration is how your body gets rid of waste.

When awake, the average adult takes about 16 breaths per minute. When asleep, that same person takes about six to eight breaths per minute.

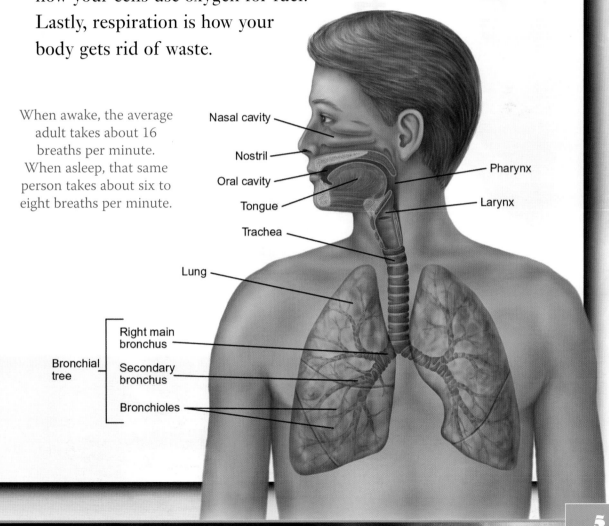

Nasal cavity

Nostril

Oral cavity

Tongue

Trachea

Lung

Bronchial tree

Right main bronchus

Secondary bronchus

Bronchioles

Pharynx

Larynx

THE NOSE AND THE SINUSES

The upper respiratory tract often starts at the nose. Sometimes it starts at the mouth, especially if the nose is blocked due to a common cold. The nose and mouth are the main doors for air to enter your body.

Most of your sinus development happens after birth. Your sinuses will be fully developed by the time you are about 20 years old.

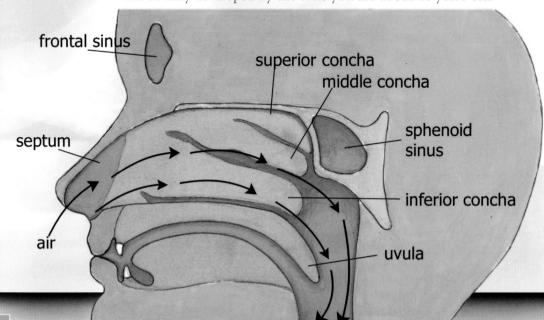

frontal sinus

superior concha

middle concha

sphenoid sinus

septum

inferior concha

air

uvula

Your nose has two openings. These are your nostrils. They lead to your nasal cavity. This hollow space is divided into two sections by your nasal septum.

Also in the nasal cavity are the nasal conchae. These bones with the funny–sounding name are your nose's heaters. As air flows by the conchae, it is warmed. Air that enters through your mouth doesn't have this luxury!

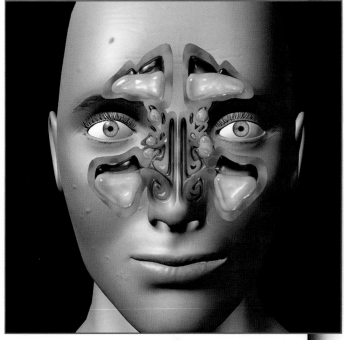

A sinus infection can cause your sinuses to fill with fluid. And, the mucous membranes may thicken.

Several more chambers open into your nasal cavity. These are called your sinuses. Sinuses are hollows in your skull. They help keep your skull light. They also affect the sound of your voice.

Sometimes, your sinuses become **infected**. When that happens, it is called **sinusitis**. This infection could be due to a common cold.

SNOT!

Short, coarse hairs grow just inside your nose. They filter particles from the air that you inhale. Mucous membrane lines the rest of the nose. The mucous membrane is loaded with blood vessels. These vessels help warm the air that passes through the nose.

Blowing your nose prevents a buildup of particles in the hairs. Be sure to wash your hands afterward so you don't spread germs.

The mucous membranes also produce a constant supply of slimy mucus that moistens and warms the air. Yep, we're talking about snot. Snot, or mucus, isn't gross when you know how important it is. Mucus keeps the lining of your airways from drying out. Without it, your insides would dry up quickly from all the passing air.

Mucus filters the air coming into your body. Have you ever blown your nose after playing in the dirt? The slimy stuff comes out black! This is all the dirt the mucus trapped and kept from entering your lungs.

The mucus on these nostril hairs traps foreign substances that you may accidentally inhale. You then blow the particles out of your nose. Or you swallow them, and they move to your stomach.

THE THROAT

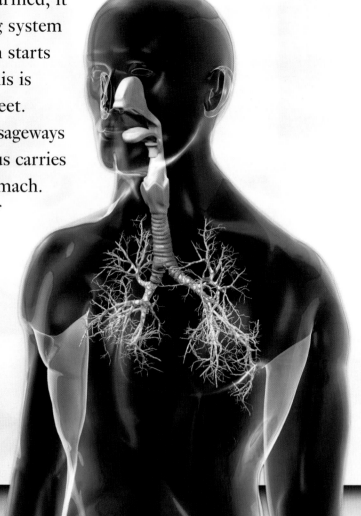

Once air is cleaned and warmed, it flows through a pretty amazing system of tunnels. This tunnel system starts at your throat, or pharynx. This is where your nose and mouth meet.

From the pharynx, two passageways open downward. The esophagus carries food from the mouth to the stomach. The trachea is for air. A flap of **cartilage** called the epiglottis covers the air tube when you swallow. This blocks food from entering the wrong tube and moving into the lungs.

Your upper respiratory tract is made up of your nose, sinuses, and pharynx. Your lower airway system is composed of your larynx, trachea, bronchi, and all of the smaller branching airways, such as the bronchioles.

The pharynx is also home to your tonsils. Tonsils make **germ** fighters to prevent respiratory **infection**. But, the tonsils often become infected and swollen. This is more common in children than adults.

A little farther down the pharynx is the voice box, or larynx. Your vocal cords are found there. Vocal cords are slitlike folds. Muscles attached to your vocal cords allow the folds to open and close. Air from your lungs causes your vocal cords to vibrate, which produces sound. This is your voice!

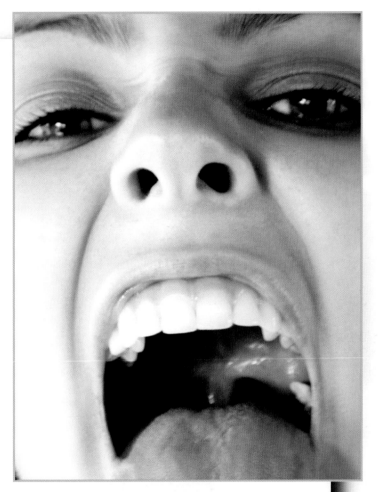

You have two tonsils at the back of your tongue. Two are at the back of your mouth. And, two are in the upper part of your throat.

THE WINDPIPE

"Hack! Cough!" Oops, did something go down the wrong tube? Sometimes food gets caught in your windpipe. This is your trachea, which was made for air only. It sits below the larynx.

The trachea is an open tube that is about five inches (13 cm) long. Strong rings of **cartilage** encircle the front part of the trachea, giving it a bumpy feel. Hairs called cilia cover the inside walls of your trachea. Like mucus, the sticky cilia grab foreign particles and keep them out of your lungs.

The larynx is about two inches (5 cm) long. Its main job is to transfer air to the trachea.

That smart epiglottis seals off your windpipe when you swallow food or liquid. This keeps the wrong things from entering your trachea.

However, sometimes food or liquid sneaks into your air tube. Coughing usually helps the foreign object get back to the right tube, the esophagus. If coughing doesn't work, a person is in danger of choking.

The Heimlich maneuver can also be used to clear a blocked larynx. To do this, apply upward pressure to the upper abdomen.

THE BRONCHIAL TREE

The trachea continues down to your chest area and divides into two tubes. At this point, your respiratory system starts to

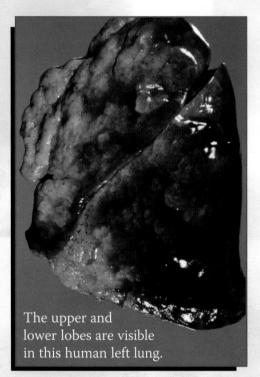

The upper and lower lobes are visible in this human left lung.

resemble an upside-down tree. In fact, it is called the bronchial tree.

The trunk of the bronchial tree is your trachea. It divides into two large airways called primary bronchi. One bronchus leads to your left lung. The other goes to the right lung.

Your left lung is made of two lobes. And, the right lung has three. The two primary bronchi divide into secondary bronchi in each of the lungs.

Secondary bronchi divide again and again until they look like skinny twigs. These airways are called bronchioles. The bronchioles end in terminal bronchioles.

Bronchioles further clean, moisten, and warm inhaled air. Then, they make sure this air reaches the gas-exchanging zone of your lungs.

The bronchial tree

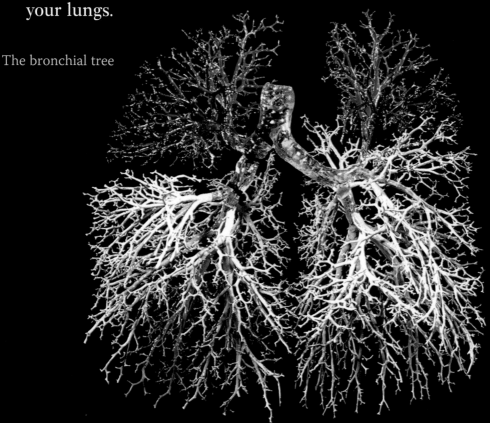

AIR SACS

Each bronchiole ends in tiny air sacs called alveoli. The alveoli sit in clusters known as alveolar sacs. The alveolar sacs look like bunches of grapes.

Alveoli have the important job of holding oxygen until it can pass into your bloodstream. Luckily, your lungs contain about 300 million alveoli for this important job. A web of tiny blood vessels, or capillaries, surrounds each cluster of alveoli. The capillary walls are very thin and **porous.**

Blood gets rid of oxygen at the same time it receives carbon dioxide. This is similar to when you trade your sandwich for your friend's apple.

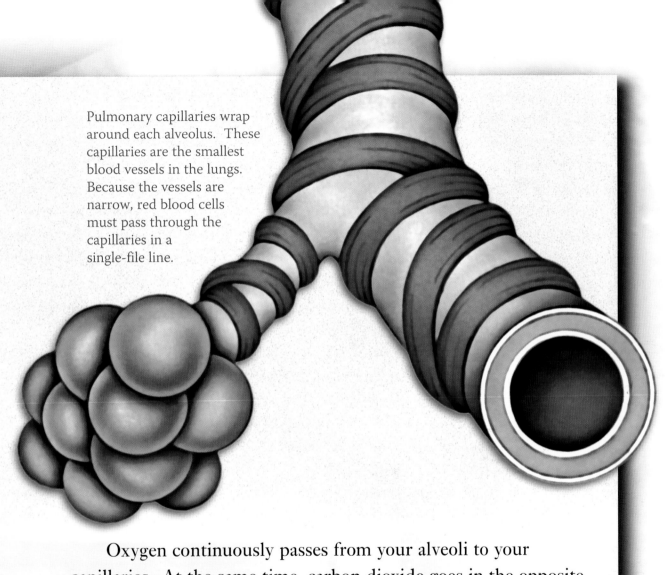

Pulmonary capillaries wrap around each alveolus. These capillaries are the smallest blood vessels in the lungs. Because the vessels are narrow, red blood cells must pass through the capillaries in a single-file line.

Oxygen continuously passes from your alveoli to your capillaries. At the same time, carbon dioxide goes in the opposite direction. It moves from the capillaries to the alveoli. From there, the carbon dioxide is exhaled from the lungs.

How We Breathe

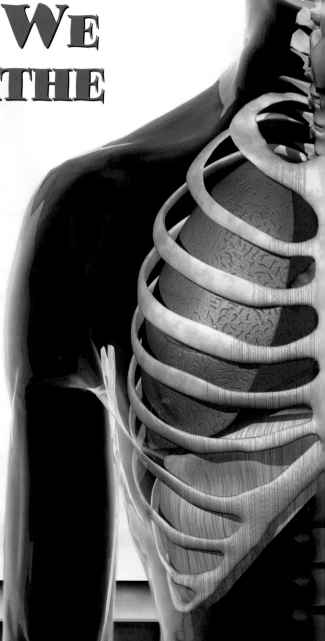

The millions of alveoli and capillaries make up a large part of your lung **tissue**. All squished together, these things make your lungs look like big, pink sponges. Each lung is about 10 to 12 inches (25 to 30 cm) long.

You learned earlier that your right lung is made of three **lobes**. It is slightly larger than your left lung. This is because your left lung shares its space with another important **organ**, your heart.

Your lungs could easily be damaged. Luckily, your rib cage and spine form a protective barrier around these delicate organs.

Beneath your lungs is the diaphragm. The diaphragm is the main respiratory muscle. This muscle helps you inhale and exhale air. When you inhale, the diaphragm flattens out and moves down. This makes more room for air in your chest cavity. When you exhale, the diaphragm relaxes and moves back up. Your chest cavity gets smaller and air is forced out.

Your diaphragm contracts when you inhale and relaxes when you exhale. When you exhale, your lungs don't completely empty. If they did, you wouldn't be able to reinflate them.

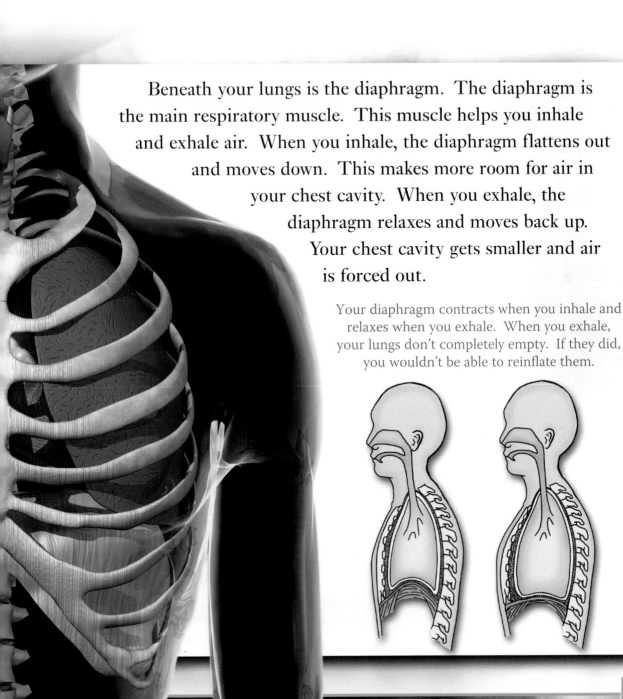

THE BIG PICTURE

It's time to put all of this together. Let's follow a molecule of oxygen through your respiratory system. We'll call this bubble of oxygen Olivia.

Olivia starts her journey at the nose. She is greeted by some tickly hairs that brush off the dirt from outside. Next, she breezes by the nasal conchae to get warmed up. She then heads down through the throat, larynx, and trachea.

Olivia decides to turn right at the base of the trachea. This takes her through a primary bronchus to the right lung. Olivia keeps moving along in the maze of smaller and smaller airways. It starts to get cramped when she reaches the bronchioles.

Suddenly, Olivia plops into an air sac. She squeezes through the air sac's wall and into a blood vessel. Whoosh, she is swept up by the bloodstream.

This begins Olivia's adventure in the circulatory system. Olivia hops onto a red blood cell. They make the journey to the heart together.

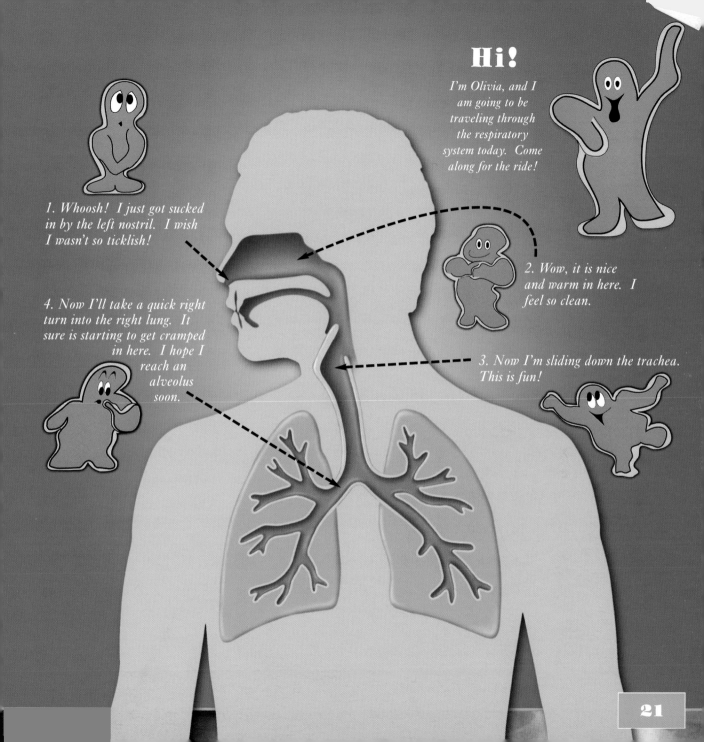

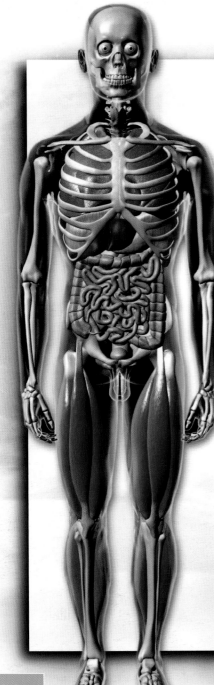

The heart's pumping gives Olivia the **momentum** needed to keep moving. Olivia swishes through the heart's left chambers. Then, she is pushed back out with great force. Together, Olivia and the blood move through larger and larger blood vessels called arteries.

You need lots of oxygen to learn all this information! So, your body decided that Olivia is needed in your brain. At the brain, Olivia jumps out of your bloodstream and into a brain cell. Along with this oxygen, your blood gives **nutrients** and fluid to your brain. This allows you to keep reading, learning, and turning these pages.

Your body could survive several days without food but only a few days without water. However, it must receive a constant supply of oxygen.

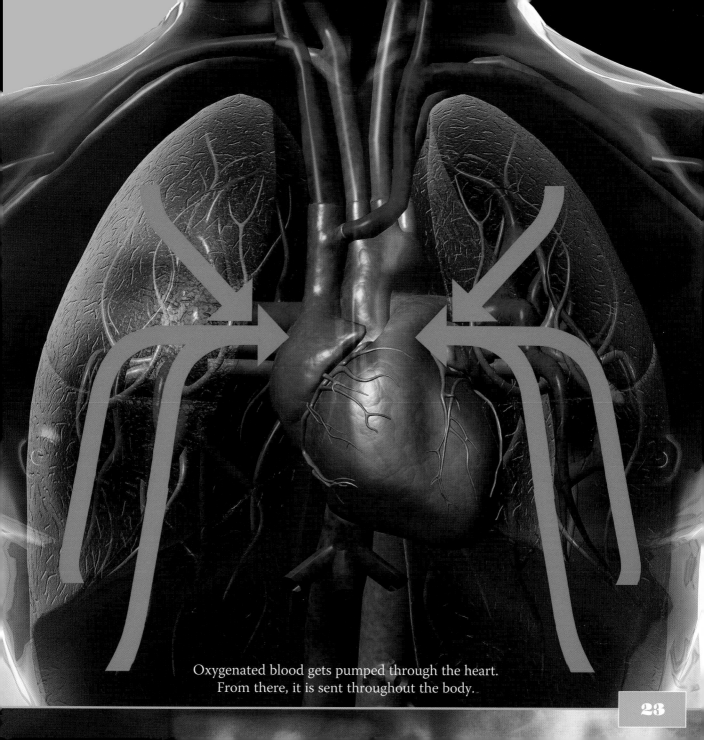

Oxygenated blood gets pumped through the heart.
From there, it is sent throughout the body.

THE RETURN TRIP

Olivia's journey is over. But, respiration creates a waste product called carbon dioxide. This gas must be removed from your body. Let's follow Charlie, a molecule of carbon dioxide, out of your body.

Charlie starts his adventure by moving out of your brain cell and into the tiny capillaries that surround it. Olivia traveled in your arteries, but Charlie travels in your veins. **Pulmonary** circulation sends Charlie through the right side of the heart. There, he gets the power needed to send him back to the lungs.

In the lungs, Charlie makes his way through smaller and smaller blood vessels. Finally, he reaches the pulmonary capillaries that surround your alveoli. Charlie passes into an air sac and begins his journey in your respiratory system.

Charlie makes his way up the bronchial tree. He travels past the larynx, through the pharynx, and out your nose or mouth. Free at last! Now, pay attention to your breathing. This entire process is happening right now with every breath you take in and let out.

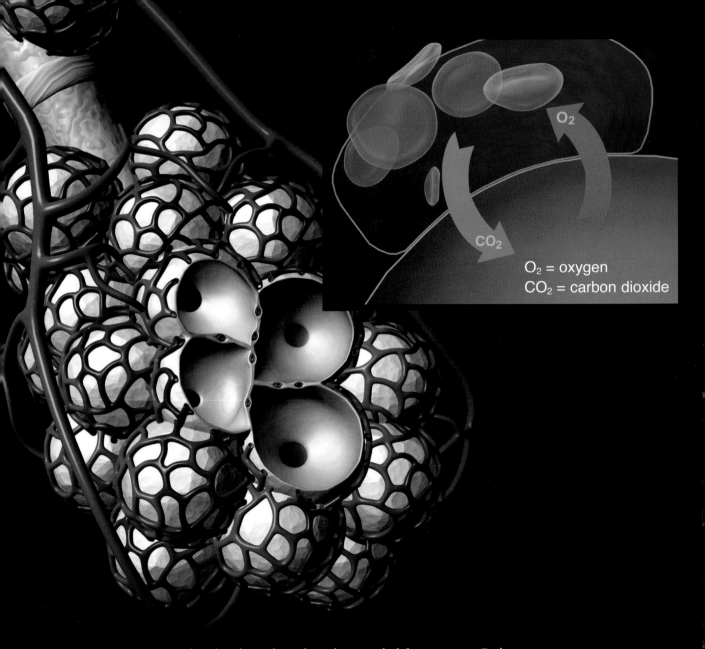

O_2

CO_2

O_2 = oxygen
CO_2 = carbon dioxide

In the alveoli, carbon dioxide is traded for oxygen. Carbon dioxide moves out of the blood and into the alveoli. At the same time, oxygen moves out of the alveoli and into the blood.

RESPIRATORY PROBLEMS

You are probably familiar with the most common respiratory **infection**. It is the common cold. A runny nose, a sore throat, or a cough are signs that a cold **virus** has invaded your respiratory system. Interestingly, these **symptoms** are not the illness itself. Coughing and sneezing force **germs** out of your airways.

A more severe form of a cold is called influenza, or the flu. The flu is a viral infection that affects either the lower or upper respiratory tracts. This may lead to pneumonia, which is a serious infection where your alveoli become filled with fluid. Then gas exchange is affected, and less oxygen is delivered to your body parts.

Asthma is a common respiratory disease. You or someone you know may have difficulty breathing due to asthma. In this condition, **irritants** in the air such as dust or mold cause the airways to narrow. Luckily, medicines can help control asthma.

Lung cancer is another disease that affects the respiratory system. Cancer cells multiply and damage the lungs and the airways. Cigarette smoking is the leading cause of lung cancer.

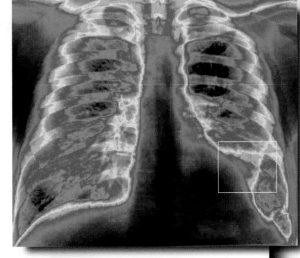

This X-ray allows us to see the cancer in this person's left lung.

During an asthma attack, smooth muscles that line the bronchi and the bronchioles tighten. This causes the airways to narrow.

Keep Your Lungs in Shape!

One way to protect your respiratory system is to not smoke. Research shows that most cases of lung cancer are related to cigarette smoking. So, just don't do it!

Why is smoking so bad for your lungs? Cigarette smoke harms the cilia in your airways. So, the little damaged hairs are less able to keep dirt and pollutants out of your lungs. As a result, a smoker is more likely to develop lung infections.

Tobacco smoke also damages the air sacs in your lungs. What does that mean? Not only is it harder just to breathe, but your whole body gets less oxygen.

There are many ways to be good to your respiratory system. Like every other part of your body, your lungs like to exercise. Running, dancing, and other fun activities make you breathe harder. This makes your lungs work their muscles and become stronger.

To avoid **infections**, wash your hands often. And, visit your doctor for regular checkups. You will breathe in and out about 20,000 times today. Be good to your respiratory system. It has a lot of work to do!

Some activities require short bursts of strength that are followed by long pauses. When you are resting, you are often left gasping for air. This is because your lungs could not supply enough oxygen to the cells.

GLOSSARY

cartilage – the soft, elastic connective tissue in the skeleton. A person's nose and ears are made of cartilage.

germ – any tiny living organism, especially one that causes disease.

infection – a disease or other harmful condition resulting from germs invading the body.

irritant – something that bothers or annoys.

lobe – a curved or rounded projection or division of a body part or an organ.

momentum – strength or force gained by motion.

nutrient – a substance found in food and used in the body to promote growth, maintenance, and repair.

organ – a part of an animal or a plant that is composed of several kinds of tissues and that performs a specific function. The heart, liver, gallbladder, and intestines are organs of an animal.

porous – capable of being passed into or through.

pulmonary – relating to the lungs.

sinusitis – inflammation of a sinus.

symptom – something that accompanies or indicates a disease or a disorder.

tissue – a group or cluster of similar cells that work together, such as a muscle.

virus – any of a large group of infective agents that are capable of growth and multiplication in living cells, and that cause various diseases.

SAYING IT

alveolus - al-VEE-uh-luhs

asthma - AZ-muh

bronchiole - BRAHN-kee-ohl

cartilage - KAHR-tuh-lihj

cilia - SIH-lee-uh

conchae - KAHN-kee

diaphragm - DEYE-uh-fram

epiglottis - eh-puh-GLAH-tuhs

esophagus - ih-SAH-fuh-guhs

larynx - LEHR-ihnks

pharynx - FA-rihnks

pneumonia - nu-MOH-nyuh

pulmonary - PUL-muh-nehr-ee

trachea - TRAY-kee-uh

WEB SITES

To learn more about the respiratory system, visit ABDO Publishing Company on the World Wide Web at www.abdopub.com. Web sites about the human body are featured on our Book Links page. These links are routinely monitored and updated to provide the most current information available.

INDEX